HUSBANDS
&
Wives

HUSBANDS
&
Wives

Liza Donnelly
and Michael Maslin

Ballantine Books • New York

Introduction and compilation copyright © 1995 by Liza Donnelly and Michael Maslin

All rights reserved under International and Pan-American Copyright Conventions. Published in the United States by Ballantine Books, a division of Random House, Inc., New York, and simultaneously in Canada by Random House of Canada Limited, Toronto.

Of the drawings in this collection, twenty-four appeared in *The New Yorker* and were copyrighted © in the years 1988 through 1993 inclusive, by *The New Yorker* Magazine, Inc.

Some of the drawings which appear in this collection originally appeared in *Good Housekeeping, New Woman, Woman, Cosmopolitan*, and *Glamour*.

Library of Congress Catalog Card Number: 94-94568

ISBN: 0-345-39041-5

Cover illustration by Michael Maslin

Manufactured in the United States of America

First Edition: February 1995

10 9 8 7 6 5 4 3 2 1

For our daughters,
Ella and Gretchen

INTRODUCTION

If you are married, have never been married, are about to be married, hope to be married, or never want to be married, you've come to the right place.

All husbands and wives have comic moments. Some of those moments slip away, while others are lovingly recalled throughout the marriage. The cartoons which follow carry you along from the first few moments of married bliss to the last, with all the thrills and spills in between. Marriage is hard work, and even though it seems headed for dead man's curve at times, at other times it seems hysterical. This book is about those catastrophic, funny times.

The two of us have been careening through marriage for seven years now. Having experienced hoards of instant in-laws, all-night "discussions," and the births of two strong-willed girls, we feel we've barely scratched the surface of marriage. The best has already happened, and yet, the best is yet to come.

—Liza Donnelly
and Michael Maslin

HUSBANDS
&
Wives

"It does come as somewhat of a surprise, Carla. I thought marriage was a roller coaster ride."

"... and you, Ralph, do you promise to ping to her every pong?"

"I know this is what you've always wanted, Ken, but I'm sorry—I want more from life than just a terrific parking space."

"I'm off to my risotto class."

"Would it surprise you to learn, Felix, that we're already married?"

"And do you, Lou-Ellen, take this man, Alex, as is?"

DONNELLY

"Nobody swirls a snifter like you, Freddie."

"I'm a people person—Roger's a sandpiper person."

"And do you promise to love, honor, and not pierce any erogenous zones till death do you part?"

"In this new life we're starting together—is there any place in particular you'd like me to sit?"

1.

2.

3.

4.

DONNELLY

". . . for richer and poorer, in sickness and in health, in bull market and bear . . ."

"You'll have to pardon Mitch—he's never been in a real marriage before."

*"In our first year of marriage we exposed
our beams, too."*

"Perhaps I haven't made myself clear. I like it when you do your Elmer Fudd voice, but I don't love it."

"See you tonight, dear. Schuss carefully."

"Louise? Are you in there?"

"Joe can't be in the same room with my crawfish étouffé."

"In order to save your marriage, we're going to need a few miracles."

"There are two men in my life. You and Harrison Ford, and not necessarily in that order."

"I thought I'd try him in there, but I'm beginning to think he works better in here."

"Not tonight, honey. The cat is in my lap."

*"The husband and wife team of Malcolm and
Evelyn Boyd."*

"I finally have the two things I wanted most in life: a swag light and a husband."

"I thought my husband and I understood each other, but then, on the very same day I switched from decaffeinated coffee to regular, he switched from regular coffee to decaffeinated."

"*Ron looks better wet than dry, just like those pretty little stones you collect along the beach.*"

"All right, I was wrong. A Shih-Tzu was not all that was missing from our marriage."

"I feel like fooling around with radicchio."

"It's our first lawsuit together."

"*I think of Lenny as my knight in shining armor,
even though he was just a guy in magenta
Bermuda shorts.*"

"*I want kids. He wants children.*"

"Our marriage is neither better nor worse since we switched to radial tires—it's just different."

"I hear their marriage is in trouble."

"I suppose if leggings found their way into our marriage, they could find their way out."

"About how many miles would you say our marriage has on it?"

*"It was surprising the first few times, Malcolm—
it isn't surprising anymore."*

"Honey, I asked you not to use the cat that way."

"This is between you and me, Harold.
Let's leave us out of it."

"*What's up, Neil? It's not like you to sit down and peel a tangelo without telling me.*"

"Unfortunately, I balance Ed the way I balance my checkbook."

"Are we tired of shiitake mushrooms yet?"

"From now on, any further communications between us will have to go through my lawyer."

OVER COORDINATED

DONNELLY

"I found the settee and Dave exactly as you see them now—I didn't have to do a thing to them."

"Some wine with your vest?"

*"Apparently they're going to stick to their story of love
at first sight."*

"Lately, his uptime has become my downtime."

"I've seen you in sickness and health, Louise, but never before in wading."

"Agreed: we'll meet downstream in about an hour."

"We have to talk, Evelyn—but not now, not here in the breakfast nook."

"I've been meaning to tell you, Herb, that your suspenders may soon put me over the edge."

"They ran out of hot dogs so I got you a tofu burger with sprouts."

"If you really want to keep the fire burning in our marriage, Edward, now would be the time to throw on a couple of logs."

"I think Maggie'll back me up on this: I don't remember our marriage ever having a theme."

"You can say 'I love you' in a half-pound to fifty-five-and-a-half pounds."

*"And another thing I like about Andrew:
he doesn't mind being left up in the air."*

"*If anything, my love for this man has grown since he appeared on 'Jeopardy.'*"

"Gut reaction?"

"For once, let's leave our ponytails out of this discussion."

"Perhaps we should begin to ask ourselves just how much more we're willing to sweep under the carpet."

*"Well, I suppose it's time we were getting back to
our husbands."*

"You could at least acknowledge the fact that I'm ignoring you."

"All right, you're sorry, you're sorry!"

"You've been sneaking in plants again."

"I feel very, very close to you, Marcia, even though we seem to be dining farther and farther apart."

"All these years you've clung to crocheted hats no matter what. I've got to admire you for that."

"I tell you, Edward—it's an away game."

*"Any objections to my throwing more light on
your apology?"*

"That's right, Phil. A separation will mean—among other things—watching your own cholesterol."

*"Are you going to offer me the beach chair, Desmond,
or will I have to take it by force?"*

"If you had been more illuminating, we wouldn't
have needed the torchère."

"I've taken him back, but I haven't taken him in."

"You had the means and the motive, but when did you have the opportunity to finish off the Linzer Torte?"

"It would help if you could stop throwing French phrases at me."

"I want him natty, but not especially nautically natty."

"It would take more than your pleats to drive us apart, but not much more."

"Does there have to be a reason—can't a husband bring his wife flowers, chocolates, and a puppy because he feels like it?"

"Harry and Beverly Smith—married for twenty-one years—are really ticked-off at each other. We'll find out if they're ready to kiss and make up right after these words from our sponsor."

*"You'd best take off your hat and coat and make
yourself comfortable, Milton. It's going to be a long,
long marriage."*

"Yes, I do remember our marriage. But more than our marriage, I remember your accessories."

"Your favorite sweater isn't here. I sent it out to be cleaned and carbon-dated."

"There's a farewell feel about you."

"I can't pinpoint it exactly, but sometime during our twenty-third year of marriage Wesley began taking notes."

"You know, honey, statistically, we should be divorced."

ABOUT THE EDITORS

MICHAEL MASLIN and LIZA DONNELLY are perhaps the only married pair of cartoonists in the country. They met *because* of cartooning. Michael Maslin has been a regular contributor to *The New Yorker* since 1978. Liza Donnelly has also been a contributor to *The New Yorker* and many other publications. For Ballantine Michael and Liza teamed to produce *Fathers and Sons*, and on her own Liza compiled and edited *Mothers and Daughters*.